MEDITATE
TO
ELEVATE

Penned from the Thoughts

of

APOSTLE COURTNEY MCLEAN

PUBLISHED BY:

Jamaica, W.I.

ISBN 978-976-96709-7-6

Cover Designed by: Geek Resource Centre
(geekjamaica@gmail.com)

Published by: Yahweh's Anointed Publishing
Tel: 876-549-0063/876-438-2256
Email: yahwehsanointedpublishing@gmail.com
Website: https://yapublishing.com

FOREWORD

Inspiration is necessary for everyday living. It encourages a positive mindset, and its application encourages change in behavior and drives action that can be life-transforming. This book offers advice from someone who has already lived through the problem you are living. These quotes offer solutions that will propel you into action as they are thought-provoking and will help you to stay focused on your life's goals. You will experience knowledge from a lifetime, condensed into just a few words to help you navigate life's challenges and shape who you are. They will increase your belief system and put your mind to work while giving you that extra boost of confidence that makes you self-assured.

Apostle Courtney Mclean has a passion for seeing transformation in the lives of God's people and he has modeled excellence in his everyday life to be an example for others to follow. This is an expression of his love for the people of God and his desire to see the manifestation of God's Divine purpose and plan for our lives realized. It will change the way you live by engaging in the application of the quotes to your lives. It will remind you of the truths about yourself that will serve you well and will help to sharpen your skills. You will be thoroughly inspired, and I trust that you will enjoy, and benefit from reading this book.

Lorraine Nelson (Maxwell Leadership Certified Coach/Speaker)

ACKNOWLEDGEMENT

I give thanks to my Lord and Saviour, Jesus Christ, who has literally taken me from the gutter through this sacred principle called Meditation.

I also give honour to Jesus Christ for the persons He has allowed me to impact. It's such a blessing to see them being selfless, inspired, and motivated enough to request my quotes and messages and then compiling them in a manner that's just genius; only requiring minimal tweaking. Thank you, Ladies Thelma, Dacia, Lorraine, and Sharon.

God bless you richly.

CONTENTS

Foreword

Acknowledgment

Introduction 7

Saturation/Surrender 11

Secret Place 15

Gifts and Talents 20

Determination 26

Development 32

Divine Help 38

Poor in Spirit 44

Poverty 50

Guard your Heart 57

Impact 62

Testimonials 67

INTRODUCTION

These thoughts/quotes came from a heart and a Spirit man that has spent a great deal of time seeking, contending with, and listening to God. While some came at a time when I was experiencing great joy, peace, and success, others came after I experienced severe pain in my soul; when there were doubts and disappointments. All through those times, God has been with me. Many times, He would give me a word that would revive my Spirit and make me want to get up and go again! Pray again! Praise again! Push again! It was out of these experiences that I would receive a theme to preach the word; where I would sense a need to pray for my people; or receive a prophetic word for my church and particular individuals. Sometimes ideas came for my business and directions for my marriage and my family. These quotes prove that in your search for God, in your waiting upon God, in your talking to and listening to God He will come through for you. He will give you a word, at the right time to suit the right occasion. Some quotes have been repeated deliberately as they align with the themes for which they are assigned.

As you read this book of quotes, don't rush through it; reflect upon what you read; savour it, speak it, live it; and most of all, use these quotes as springboards to be inspired to create your own quotes from the depths of your soul.

I believe this book has come at a time when it is needed. We are living in a time when anything goes; where people, especially young people, don't seem to have thoughts of their own but are easily swayed by what they see on Social Media; or they follow the "herd" wherever it moves.

When God told Joshua to take over the leadership from Moses, the major principle that Joshua needed for success was meditation. Joshua was from a culture of slavery while Moses was from a culture of royalty. For Joshua to successfully take on his new mission, he needed to meditate, so he could elevate his thinking. Most of what happens in life are determined by our mindset. Proverbs 4:23 (NLT) declares, "Guard your heart above all else, for it determines the course of your life." So Joshua had to reset his heart and his mind through the principle of meditation. Meditation is a master key that has the potential to transform and elevate one's life.

To meditate means to:

Muse
Mutter
Utter
and Growl

Muse

Begin to imagine what God says about you. This is using your imagination in a positive way. You become so absorbed in thought; you begin seeing what you think about the inside of you.

Mutter

Speak it under your breath! Speak it to yourself! You are working on convincing yourself that what you see inside of you is not true. You are reprogramming your subconscious and reconstructing the new man; the one God created you to be.

Utter

Speak it into the atmosphere! They'll realize that the man they once knew is gone. This is the new you! The elevated you! Don't let them push you back! The growl is coming, which is strong enough to not be pushed back.

Growl

Like a lion stamping his authority in the jungle! With a loud authoritative tone, declare that you are this new man; and watch your life elevate.

As you use this master key to reprogram your life, begin to see it (muse), mutter it, utter it and growl it. You will meditate and then elevate. To elevate is to lift or move to a higher or more important level. It's time!!!! The time for your lifting is now!

It's your time to think; it's your time to listen to what God is saying to you. It's your time to release what God has spoken into your spirit.

Grace and peace be yours.

Apostle Courtney McLean

SATURATION/SURRENDER

Saturation/Surrender is experienced through the extensive, exclusive, earnest pursuit of "soaking in God's presence." It encompasses a persistent desire of advancement from a casually carnal to a saturated Spiritual life. It is sincerely asking God to "Visit my life."

Scriptural References: James 4:8; Psalm 1:2; Romans 8:1, 4, 9

QUOTES:

- You will never experience elevation until your soul is under subjection.
- Once you lose your thirst you have lost your river.
- Until the pursuit of His presence becomes your priority you are practicing idolatry.
- Do not trust a heart that is not bathed in prayer, even if it is yours.
- Never trust emotions that have not been subdued and saturated in His presence.

- His helping presence does not visit your life. He abides in you.
- Transformation comes through encounters.
- Your marriage will become exemplary when you wash each other with the Word of God.
- Develop prophetic action that will induce manifestation.

📖📖📖📖📖📖📖📖📖📖📖

As a Christian, do you aim for saturation/surrender on a daily basis or as often as possible?

Why should Saturation/Surrender be a priority?

____

____

____

____

____

____

____

____

____

What changes or revelations have you seen in your walk with God since your Saturation/Surrender experience?

____

____

____

____

____

____

____

____

____

Which of the above is/are your "stand out" quote(s)? State why.

How will you apply this message from the quotation to your life?

THE SECRET PLACE

The Secret Place is a sacred place, the holy presence of Almighty God. It is intense intercession that connects you to the Secret Place. One cannot live a spiritually uplifting life or be endowed with the anointing, without waiting (dwelling) in the Secret Place.

Scriptural References: Psalm 27:5, Psalm 91:1, Nahum 1:7

QUOTES

- No adversity will prevent my intimacy.
- Rest begins with prayer.
- As of today I make spiritual maturity my priority.
- The anointing comes when, after the laying on of hands, you find the secret place and stay there; then call upon the Lord...waiting.
- We appropriate the anointing in the secret place.

- Babies are developed in the womb; butterflies are developed in the cocoon; the anointing is developed in the secret place.
- Even if I lay hands on you publicly, you must appropriate anointing privately.
- The anointing comes when you are consistent despite the disappointment, betrayal, and trouble.
- The transference initiates but the secret place appropriates.

□□□□□□□□□□□□□□□□□□

How important is the Secret Place to you?

____

____

____

____

____

____

____

____

____

How often do you dwell in your Secret Place?

Where is your Secret Place?

Explain the experience of being there.

Name the Spiritual weapon that is available in the Secret Place and say how this helps you.

Which of the above is/are your "stand out" quote(s)? State why.

How will you apply the message(s) from the quotation(s) to your life?

GIFTS AND TALENTS

How do you get to that expected end that is promised for God's children? By using your gifts and talents! We are advised though, to consult the Lord before stepping out and allow Him to daily order your steps. Plan ahead, continue seeking and soaking in His presence. This is how you will learn how you are meant to impact your world. There is a 'you' inside of you that you need to discover. Another way to assist in unearthing your gifts and talents is to see how you fare in hard situations. How you navigate through them can help you to discover a gift you never knew you had. You can also ask others because many times it is people who help us to see the gifts and talents with which God has blessed us. People you admire are very good at helping you to discover what you have. List their gifts/talents and then check to see what you have in common. The Lord will always lead you to the right persons to provide the needed support. Spend time in the Word and heed the word of the Lord. It provides clarity.

Scriptural References: Matthew 25: 14-30; Ephesians 2:10

QUOTES

- It is an insult to your Creator to underestimate the talents and gifts that He has deposited in you.
- It is an insult to your Creator to underutilize your gifts and not maximize your potential.
- Think with ink, empty your thoughts on paper, then prioritize.
- Manage your time in seconds not minutes
- If you don't do the action plan, you are just going through the motions.
- Whatever sacrifice I make, I make it with the redemptive work of Jesus in mind.
- Idealization without manifestation leads to frustration.
- To step into your purpose, you must fight ignorance.

- I am awesome, Nobody is better than I am!
- Humility is Teach-ability.

What do you think your gift(s) is/are?

What are your talents?

How did you realize your gifts and talents?

Have you ever worked with a coach/mentor? How has this person helped you to recognize what you have inside (gift)?

What are the gifts/talents you admire in your coach/mentor? What similarities, if any, have you noticed between you?

"There is a 'you' inside of you that you need to discover" What do you understand from this expression?

Which of the above is/are your "stand out" quote(s)? State why.

How will you apply this message from the quotation to your life?

DETERMINATION

Determination is the quality of being firm with your purpose. "Dream big, start small, act now," is a quote from Robin Sharma. Our dreams are supposed to be so big that they scare us and pull us out of our comfort zone. Comfort zones are cushions; places where we plateau and settle; where we sometimes believe we are happy. So why dream? Our dreams help to push us towards intentionally accomplishing our purpose. They help us to defeat the imposter within us to overcome limiting beliefs. I invited the members of my church to submit a list of 22 things each wished to accomplish for the year. Had you taken on such a task, how determined would you be to get those things done? You must position yourself so that whenever contradictions come, you are ready! Your determination means you approach life with intentionality, because, without it, retraction takes place. Know that you have a call on your life, and there is always going to be a contradiction with that call, but be resolute, and don't faint in the contradiction. Determination is one of the D's needed to survive during your lifetime, and certainly should be on your to-do list at the beginning of a year.

Scriptural References: Colossians 3:23; 1 Corinthians 10:31; Titus 2: 7-8

QUOTES

- Your desire to live and overcome must be stronger than the devil's desire to kill you.
- Determination and discipline help you to go beyond your feelings.
- Faith is: walking it, talking it, believing it, until you become it.
- In an age of distraction, it is important to crystalize your vision.
- The action of faith is characterized by a stretch.
- Affirmation without deliberate action leads to frustration.

- The anointing comes when you are consistent despite the disappointment, betrayal, and trouble.
- Don't say why it can't, ask how it can.
- When you are fighting with your warped foundation it requires grit and determination to break out.

Spend some time reflecting now and share a goal or dream that you were determined to accomplish and did. Share the process.

What is/are your current goal(s)/dream(s)? How determined are you to accomplish this/them?

____

____

____

____

____

____

____

____

____

With your current goal(s)/dream(s), on a scale of 1-5; with 5 being the greatest determining factor; where would you place your determination level? What are you prepared to do to increase this level?

____

____

____

____

____

____

____

Have you ever had a dream that scares you? If so, what is that dream?

Which of the above is/are your "stand out" quote(s)? State why.

How will you apply this message from the quotation to your life?

___

___

___

___

___

___

___

___

___

___

___

DEVELOPMENT

At the beginning of a year, we tend to evaluate our lives to see what areas need improvement. Maybe you believe it's time you get that house you have been dreaming about; maybe it's a new car, a new skill, or higher education. It could be getting a new and better-paying job to adequately provide for you and your family. At the beginning of every year, we should aim to develop ourselves so we will be closer to realizing our goals and dreams. Development is intrinsic to success!

Our development should be considered a Spiritual process. How do we make that needed Spiritual assessment and improvement? It is a process, accomplished by seeking after and soaking in the presence of the Lord thus building a relationship with Him. In seeking Him first above everything else, we renew our minds. As we present our bodies to doing His will, we are mentally transformed into appreciating the 10/90 Principle, that is, life is 10% what happens to you and 90% how you respond to it. We learn how to discern the Lord's directives on the exact steps to take toward a Christ-like self-development. Development is another of the D's needed to survive during your lifetime, and certainly should be on your to-do list at the beginning of a year.

Scriptural References Romans 12: 1- 2; 1 Peter 4: 10-11

QUOTES

- Your misery will develop your ministry.
- When you know and grow you begin to show.
- The storm is not here to kill you; it comes to build you. Stay calm.
- To step into your purpose, you must fight ignorance.
- If you don't fast, you won't last.
- Every adversity comes with an opportunity to build importunity, thus causing ascendancy.
- Idealization without manifestation leads to frustration.

z□□□□□□□□□□□□□□□□□□□□

What are the areas of development on which you are working? What plans have you put in place to develop these areas?

How far are you with those plans?

How do you feel about your development and your current stage in life? What is/are the reason(s) for this?

How committed are you to staying on track with your development?

____

____

____

____

____

____

____

____

Which of the above is/are your "stand out" quote(s)? State why.

____

____

____

____

____

____

____

____

____

How will you apply this message from the quotation to your life?

DIVINE HELP

How do you step out of the boat into that which scares you? You step out KNOWING that the Lord has already provided a way. You step out because you have an awareness of the presence of God in your life and in the lives of His people. This is Divine help. This is where we recognize that with God's help, we can and will succeed. When you are properly aligned with the Lord, He is better able to pour into your life and strengthen you. The help we receive is never just for us; we are expected to pour into other people's lives; help them to see beyond how they see themselves. We need to show them the love and grace that comes only from God.

We who are believers will contend that we cannot do anything successfully without Divine help; as proven in the following Scriptures:-

Philippians 4:13 - I can do all things through Christ who strengthens me.

Ps 32: 6 & 7 - Therefore every loyal person

should pray to you in time of distress. Though flood waters threaten, they will never reach him. You are my shelter; you guard me from distress; with joyful shouts of deliverance, you surround me.

Is 58: 9 - Then you will call, and the LORD will answer your cry for help, and he will say: Here am I.

Romans 9: 16 - It does not, therefore, depend on human desire or effort, but on God's mercy.

God has used me to do mighty exploits. I have seen cancers healed, the lame walk, the deaf hear, mental imbalance and marriages restored. Were it not for Divine help, none of these would have happened. Divine help is the final of the 3 D's I believe is necessary for survival during one's lifetime. Please know that this is not unique to me. His gift is freely given.

Other Scriptural References: Isaiah 41:10, 13; Matthew 5: 14- 16

QUOTES

- Stop crying over what God has already resurrected.
- God will bring people into your life who will connect with you, not because of what you have but because of what you carry.
- You are the creation of an awesome Creator.
- God wants to take you from restless to stressless.
- You are going to be paid for your shame.
- Live by design and not by crisis.
- Authorized to neutralize.

Have you ever had an experience where, based on the situation/circumstances, it was only Divine help that could have brought you through? Please share this experience

____

____

____

____

What is your current situation for which you need Divine help? If you consider it personal and confidential, you may give a general statement.

Briefly recount your favourite story in the Bible where Divine help was received. Give the Scriptural reference.

Mention a situation where God used you as Divine help to someone.

Which of the above is/are your "stand out" quote(s)? State why.

____

How will you apply this message from the quotation to your life?

____

POOR IN SPIRIT

To be "poor in spirit" has been given several meanings as persons attempt to give their personal thoughts on the meaning of this Scriptural expression. This is where the different versions of the Bible on this text become very important and appreciated. I believe the New Living Translation (NLT) offers a clear idea of the meaning of "poor in spirit". It states, "...those who are poor and realize their need for him." (Matthew 5:3)

The poor in spirit is the one who sees himself as being in need of Spiritual help.

He understands his help comes from the Lord.

Psalm 121:1 states, "I will lift up mine eyes unto the hills..." because I understand that as powerful as I am, there are limitations. However, I don't need to be overwhelmed by them; I just need to understand from where my help comes. It comes from the Limitless One

My limitations don't need to lead to degradation

because I look to God. That recognition of my limitation may now lead to elevation.

"Blessed are the poor in spirit for theirs is the kingdom of Heaven" (KJV)

Scriptural References: Matthew 5:3; Matthew 5:6

QUOTES

- Wherever you complain you remain. Whenever you praise you are raised.
- Until my spirituality has become my priority I'll never rise from religious mediocrity.
- Priority of spirituality is revealed by the investment of time, treasure, and energy.
- Idealization without manifestation leads to frustration.
- Discouragement comes when you focus on the container above the content.
- Confront and change that negative character or you circulate it.
- Our lack of value for spiritual things has led to our demise.

Highlight a situation in the Bible where a Character could be described as being “poor in spirit”

Describe a point in your life where you believe you were “poor in spirit”

____

____

____

____

____

____

____

____

____

Name some strategies that may be employed to get out of Spiritual poverty.

____

____

____

____

____

____

____

____

____

____

Is there a commonality between the two Scriptural references above? If yes, please state. If there is nothing in common, why do you say so?

____

____

____

____

____

____

____

____

____

Which of the above is/are your “stand out” quote(s)? State why.

____

____

____

____

____

____

____

____

How will you apply this message from the quotation to your life?

POVERTY

Do you consider yourself in poverty or enjoying prosperity? When you think of your current financial state, do you believe it's God's plan for your life? If you are currently employed, is your salary able to manage all your responsibilities? If not, would you then consider yourself in poverty? God's plan for you is not poverty, but that you will "prosper and be in good health even as your soul prospereth" (3 John 1:2 KJV). Here are a few sure ways of rejecting poverty:

1. Work more on internal prosperity and the results will show outwardly.
2. Associate with persons who are functioning at levels you admire/can emulate.
3. Develop the heart of a student by consistently asking questions at the appropriate time.
4. Shift your heart (Work on changing the state of your heart).

5. Shift your mind (Change your mindset/reset your mindset).

Then you'll see a change in your life.

Proverbs 18:12 states, "Before destruction the heart of man is haughty, and before honour is humility."

Poverty leads to destruction and it's preceded by pride.

Honour leads to prosperity and it's preceded by humility.

Humility is Teachability

As ironic as it sounds, you "destroy" poverty by not seeing yourself as poor.

So start giving – "Bring ye all the tithes into the storehouse, that there may be meat in mine house, and prove me now herewith, saith the Lord of hosts, if I will not open you the windows of heaven, and pour you out a blessing, that there shall not be room enough to receive it." (Malachi 3:10)

To change this particular situation in your life, you need a God strategy. As you do the will of the Lord concerning your job and your finances; seek Him to give you a strategy for your liberation.

Scriptural References: Psalm 34: 5-6; 1 Samuel 2: 8

QUOTES

- Poor people are the proudest set of people on earth, that's why they are poor.
- Prosperity begins with frugality.
- Destruction is generally preceded by ignorance and pride.
- Poverty is connected to illiteracy.
- Whatever sacrifice I make, I make it with the redemptive work of Jesus in mind.
- The action of faith is characterized by a stretch.

- Never seek today's fun while forfeiting tomorrow's fortune.

How much do you believe the Malachi reference mentioned above (Malachi 3:10)?

Have you ever had a Malachi 3:10 experience? Briefly share it.

____

____

____

____

____

____

____

____

____

After reading this section, how do you now feel about poverty?

____

____

____

____

____

____

____

____

____

____

After reading and reflecting, what strategy do you sense God is giving you for defeating poverty?

____

____

____

____

____

____

____

____

____

Which of the above is/are your "stand out" quote(s)? State why.

____

____

____

____

____

____

____

____

____

How will you apply this message from the quotation to your life?

GUARD YOUR HEART

Blood is a life-giving commodity. Without it we cannot live as within the blood lies the oxygen we need to survive. Without blood, we wouldn't be able to fight infections or rid our bodies of waste matter. It is the heart that pumps blood within our bodies; so the heart may be regarded as the most vital organ. We can therefore understand and appreciate when the Bible says, "Guard your heart...for it determines the course of your life." (Proverbs 4:23 NLT). 'Guard your heart' means to protect it or to prevent negative thoughts from entering, then dwelling there. Instead, we should aim to cherish or process the thoughts which are worthy of positive action and not destruction. The kinds of seeds we sow in our hearts will determine the fruits we produce. What seeds are you sowing? What fruits are you producing? Remember that man looketh on the outward appearance but only God truly sees the heart. Therefore, make sure your heart is right with God. Just like your regular medical checks, you need to schedule time for a Spiritual ECG.

Scriptural References: Psalm 51:10; Proverbs 4:23; Luke 6:45

QUOTES

- Your addiction to distraction causes death to your creative ability.
- The state of your heart determines what you see.
- Your progression is in your gratitude.
- Do not allow the enemy to distract, dislocate and destroy you.
- If you want extraordinary results then you must be extraordinary.
- Fear tolerated is faith contaminated.
- As long as you haven't gotten over it, you are a slave to it.
- If you don't fast, you won't last.
- Could the leprosy be caused by your familiarity and irreverence for that which is sacred?

What are some of the issues of life from which you need to guard your heart?

____

____

____

____

____

____

____

____

____

____

What strategies have you put in place to guard your heart?

____

____

____

____

____

____

____

____

"The state of your heart determines what you see" How do you interpret this?

Besides the one above, which of the above is/are your "stand out" quote(s)? State why.

How will you apply this message from the quotation to your life?

IMPACT

The theme of our church for 2021/2022 was "Strengthening the Core for Global Impact." Our aim is for personal revival, household revival, church revival, national revival, and global impact. The essence of impact is demonstrating positive, intentional actions/morals that influence/inspire people to change or improve. We must never stop growing because there are people waiting on us to put a positive spin on their lives. These people were born to win but have been cultured or wired to fail. It is our job therefore to re-wire them for winning at life. They need to know that they were 'Wired to Win[1]. We should be remembered long after the transition, for the impact we created.

Scriptural References: Matthew 5:13-16; Matthew 28:19; Philippians 2:3.

---

[1] Wired to Win Productivity Planner Available at the Bookstore (WAFIF) & on Amazon.

QUOTES

- I refuse to be good for nothing, someone must feel my impact.
- Leave the herd of victims and join the circle of champions.
- Impact is living with the mentality of intentionality. Without this, you become a casualty and liability.
- Write your signature in history through your impact.
- Compassion unlocks power.
- Don't be confused, it's your time to shine!
- Cry out for revival. Let God use you, revive you; give you a passion that's unstoppable!
- Don't reject...accept. Let people feel the love even if their actions are not yet aligned.
- Culture is more seeing than saying.

How intentional have you been about impacting lives?

____

Share an experience where you made an impact on a person's life

Explain how creating impact can serve the giver and the receiver.

Which of the above is/are your "stand out" quote(s)? State why.

How will you apply this message from the quotation to your life?

TESTIMONIALS

"Apostle Courtney McLean's book of Inspirational Quotes is a plethora of phrases and pronouncements. These are quotes that possess the power to pull you into pensive places and prepare you for perspectives that will set you on your path to productivity and purpose. They explore the spontaneity of the venerable Apostle's spirituality, as they are excerpts from his manifold masterful messages that have been manifesting his mission to impact lives globally. The quotes are appropriate to life's daily challenges and more importantly, will stimulate you to create solutions that are indicative of their substantial value. Apostle McLean's signature is not only written in history but I dare say, etched in history"

Sharon Gray; member of Worship and Faith International Fellowship (WAFIF)

"I would recommend this book to anyone at whatever stage of the life process called Christianity. It offers little jolts of wisdom needed for our big dreams and a fresh look at the things that have become familiar. Many are gifted with unearthed talents and there are quotes here that may just be the key needed to cause those talents to be manifested. I kept looking at myself and still saw the old me and that hindered me, but the quote that said "It is an insult to your Creator to underestimate the talents and the gifts that He has deposited in you" was my key. I was looking at myself when my focus needed to be on God. He has already provided all my victories."

Dacia Bent-Wilson; member of Worship and Faith International Fellowship

"I have seen and heard of many books of quotes. However, this is one with a difference. I like the fact that it is divided into sections with themes/subheadings supported by quotes relevant to these themes. So instead of searching for a quotation that suits my situation, which can be a tedious process; I simply check the themes that would envelop what my emotions are communicating to me, and then choose a quote that is suitable to that emotional and Spiritual need. Rest assured the quotes are so many and varied, I guarantee you will find one which resonates with you. Based on his previous works, it is fair to conclude that Apostle Courtney McLean has the growth of his followers and supporters at heart. They are excellent books and this is no exception. I recommend it highly."

Thelma Porter; Coach, Mentor, Speaker, Leadership Trainer; Head of the Communications Ministry, Worship and Faith International Fellowship

www.ingramcontent.com/pod-product-compliance
Lightning Source LLC
LaVergne TN
LVHW010120170826
845678LV00012B/2510

* 9 7 8 9 7 6 9 6 7 0 9 7 6 *